'I am the true vine and my father is the vinedresser. Every branch in me that bears no fruit he will take away; and every branch that bears fruit he will cleanse, that it may bear more fruit.' John 15: 1

Fr. Damasus Winzen, O.S.B.
Prior

Mount Saviour

Nov. 24, 1956
Feast of St. John of the Cross

Symbols of Christ

THE OLD TESTAMENT · THE NEW TESTAMENT

BY

DAMASUS WINZEN, O.S.B.

DRAWINGS BY WILLIAM V. CLADEK

P. J. KENEDY & SONS

NEW YORK

IMPRIMI POTEST
* BERNARDUS KAELIN
Abbas Primas, O.S.B.
die 10a augusti, 1955.

NIHIL OBSTAT
Rucupis, die xvi mensis augusti, anno MCMLV
WILFREDUS T. CRAUGH
Censor Deputatus

IMPRIMATUR
Rucupis, die xviii mensis augusti, anno MCMLV
* JACOBUS EDUARDUS
Episcopus Roffensis in America

246
WI5

Foreword

AN ALLEGORY is a rationally contrived thing like the famous three hares in the circular window of Paderborn Cathedral which are arranged in a circle in such a fashion that they chase each other joined by the ears. Thus they have three ears in common, which, of all things, is meant to "symbolize" the unfathomable mystery of mysteries: the Most Holy Trinity. Such an allegory "explains" nothing but admits imagination where imagination has no place and where the mind should accept silence. Unless you are trained in medieval allegorism and are a good guesser, you would neither think a hare fit to represent a Divine Person, nor three of these unheroic beasts a better help than the word Trinity in all its bareness.

There must be a place for the playfulness of allegory, or how else could we have so much of it: allegorism in the exegesis of the Old and New Testament, allegorism wreaking havoc in the explanation of the liturgy, allegorism in philosophy, in patriotic emblems and finally a burst of allegorism of the most arbitrary kind in such secret, fraternal organizations as the Rosicrucians, Masons and their imitators. Some of it is outright silly, some misleading.

Leon Bloy it was, I think, who created the term *niaiseries sulpiciennes* with no reference to the church or the good and learned Fathers of St. Sulpice. He rather meant the shops that flourish around the square on which the church stands and their "ecclesiastical hardware." One of the *niaiseries sulpiciennes* is what so many good, religious people take for a "symbol" of the Holy Eucharist or Mass: a book over which a priest's stole is draped, upon it a chalice, and, floating freely in the air above the rim of the sacred beaker, a host, unleavened, perhaps surrounded by the rays of a sunburst. One might question whether or not this is even an allegory, as it is so obvious that it could not claim to be taken for anything else but a photographic picture of a few of the things needed for Mass, but it certainly is not a symbol.

And here is the heart of the matter: what is to be represented is already *the* symbol, so that this symbol is a "symbol" of a symbol. Wine and bread are symbols of Christ, as the book is. True, they are infinitely higher in the order of symbols because they contain in a sacramental, yet most real, way what they symbolize: the Word of God, the Sacrifice of Redeeming Blood, the Body of the Lamb slain for us.

Before an unknown priest of the fourteenth century, long after the introduction of the Feast of Corpus Christi and far from Rome, in the city of Danzig, put one of the sacred species into a reliquary, which thus became the ancestor of our monstrance, the tendency of Catholics was not to expose but to veil in mercy what the eye can never fathom: the altar was veiled, the ciborium was veiled, the sacred "bread basket" (or tabernacle) was veiled, the chalice was veiled and so were gospel book and paten. Even now a veil is used for sacramental benediction.

These considerations could be extended, but let us not digress further: the true symbol is like a veil concealing the outline of the thing symbolized: bread, water, oil, wine, incense, candles; fire, a rise, a tree, a river; hands, outstretched or folded; prostration, bowing and kneeling; white linen, rich silk and precious stones; in short, the simple, given things of social or solitary natural life fitted by the mind—*logos,* Word—to be endowed with a unique and appropriate sense.

Why did God choose Sinai, Zion, Horeb and Moria, Golgotha and Thabor to manifest himself to man? Because a rise, heaven above symbolize to man—more erect than other creatures, carrying his forehead like a banner of reason—the Power of Light, while the soil in all religions bears in itself the signification of dark, telluric, chthonic forces—as long as we stay within the realm of symbol and do not lapse into paganism or rank superstition. The Catholic Church is drenched and soaked in symbolism—with a generous shot of allegorism added by the playful and rationalistic Middle Ages, alas!—and it could not be otherwise, since the very Incarnation, the Becoming Man of God, is in its deepest meaning a symbol of *agape,* God's outflowing love. But Catholics have been to a very great extent blinded to symbols and have lost the sense of the analogical which would

5

keep us aware of the basic fact that all our wordy definitions are not even approximations of reality, but analogies.

And so we have become sightless toward the infinite objects of our faith and are busy with its nearby mechanics: we don't see the face and hands of the clock, but are forever busy with its cogs and wheels, forgetting that it might stop if we continue to take it apart.

This book, together with Father Damasus' great work, *Pathways in Holy Scripture*, is an eye opener. As when one approaches a mountain range in the sun, its peaks and chasms assume names and shapes when the green plateau is eaten up mile after mile, so the figures, images and persons of both Testaments become familiar and point out the Son of Man. The Burning Bush, the Serpent of Bronze, the Rising Sun, Moses and Elias, and a hundred more raise their voices to chant and sing him. They do this spontaneously or they fail: if there is the wrong start and the cerebration precedes the vision, we have sterile and contrived allegorism. Nor does it help worship and liturgy if the symbol is too alien and mediate.

As bread, wine, oil and candles of wax, and not wheat, grapes, olives and beehives are used as vehicles of divine significance, the dionysiac element of the mystery cults is taken away and man as *cives* and shaper enters into the sphere of the creator. Only water and fire, both purifiers, are used in their raw and natural state. This indicates how deeply Christianity is committed to history, to civilization, to interplay of infinite Creator and finite creature, to Word and Spirit.

This little book is, therefore, of great importance for a sober and truly reasonable comprehension of Word and Sacrament, Scripture and liturgy. The naturalism and "photographism" in our Church art, the unrelatedness to the mystery in the furnishings even of the sanctuary, cry out for symbolism. The feasts, the Church year, all the Masses, baptism, their renewal in the hour-chant cry for the more allusive art of the symbol. Our churches symbolize the meeting of man and God, a sacramental *parousia*, a piercing of the soul by the sword of the Word: therefore the air needs to be filled with the fragrance of Christ, which like a sweet odor, demands the subtle and delicate, the allusive means of the symbol.

H. A. REINHOLD

Carmel-by-the-Sea
Solemnity of St. Benedict
1955

Contents

Contents

Introduction

THE WORD "symbol" is derived from the Greek word *symballein*, which means "to piece together." According to a widespread custom in Greco-Roman antiquity, the host broke a potsherd, or a ring, and gave one half to his guest, while he retained the other half. When the guest returned, the one half of the potsherd fitting into the other proved him a guest of the house with the right of hospitality. The "symbol" gave him a home.

God has created this visible world as a "symbol," as the one half of the potsherd; his Divine Wisdom, that was with him as his master workman when he marked the foundations of the earth, being the other half. Then God fashioned man from the dust of the earth and breathed into him His Spirit; He created him as a living symbol, body and mind fitting together. In man's body, the whole visible world was gathered together. His mind was a likeness of God's Eternal Wisdom. "God created man from the earth . . . and set his eye upon their hearts to show them the greatness of his works" (Ecclus. 17:1,7). It was man's task to fit the whole world to God's Wisdom, and thus prove himself at home in God's house, by searching out the essence of things as signs of God's Wisdom and lifting them up in praise and thanksgiving to their Creator. When he yielded to the temptation of the serpent and wanted to be wiser than God, "his eyes were opened," as it is said ironically in Holy Scripture (Gen. 3:7), "and he saw, not God, but himself, that he was naked." From then on, what was to be is said in the book Ecclesiastes (3:11): "God has made everything beautiful in its time. He has set the world into man's heart, yet man cannot find out the work that God has done from the beginning even to the end." Man had ceased to be a living symbol. Henceforth, he would be unable to fit the two parts of the potsherd together; the visible things would no longer act as windows through which the light of God's Wisdom would fall into his heart. "Hearing they hear and understand not: and see visions and know it not" (Isa. 6:9). Man lived no more in this world as a guest in God's home, but as a stranger in an inn.

"O God, thou hast rejected us, thou hast broken our battle lines, thou hast been angry, do thou restore us. Thou hast shaken the earth, hast rent it: heal its breaches, for it is tottering. Thou hast laid hard trials upon thy people, thou hast made us drink of a heady wine. *Thou hast given a banner to them that* fear thee, to which they may flee from before the bow" (Ps. 59:1–4). In the midst of a world that had lost its peace by forfeiting its meaning as a symbol of the Divine Wisdom, God left a *sign* to the faithful remnant of those who feared him; the sign of the Messias. Appearing in various forms through the centuries of the Old Covenant, it kept alive the hope for the restoration of all things in a New Adam, who would heal the breaches by fitting together again the two parts of the potsherd. In Jesus Christ, in whom the Word became flesh, this hope is fulfilled; he is the Perfect Symbol. In him, all things, those that are above and those that are beneath the human nature and the divine nature, are fitted together into the one Divine Person of the Son of God. When he arose from the dead, he gave the light of a new understanding into the hearts of his disciples, "that they might understand the Scriptures. . . . And beginning with Moses and all the prophets he expounded unto them in all the Scriptures the things concerning himself" (Luke 24:45, 27). All those who are incorporated into him become themselves a part of this Living Symbol, the Lord Jesus Christ. This Spirit enlightens them. They recognize the signs of the Messias that God had set up in various ways throughout the centuries in the Old Testament, and they interpret them in the light shed upon them by the clearer signs of the New Testament.

Through his symbols, the Risen Saviour exercises continuously his healing, integrating, illuminating power in the faithful. The symbols of Christ are more than a clever means to convey an idea through external signs; they are a means to share in the life of the Saviour in such a way that the whole being of man is involved. Take the first of the symbols of Christ, the Cross. It never was a mere illustration of an abstract truth. We find it long before Christ, all over the world, held in great esteem as a "sacramental," that represented and caused the wholeness of life because it seemed to gather unto itself the entire universe. This sacramental character of the Cross remains in the Christian use of the symbol. We not only look at, but we *make* the sign of the cross as a blessing, not for some "magical" reason. It represents the life-giving death of Christ, and leads us into "the breadth, the length, the depth and height" of the love of Christ (cf. Eph. 3:18).

All the symbols explained in these pages represent the *fullness* of the salvation wrought by Christ. They are not limited to one particular aspect of the Lord's work. They comprehend the whole history of redemption, joining the beginning to the end. From the texts given underneath each, the reader can easily see how these symbols of the Messias are like red threads going through and binding together into a marvelous unity both the Old and the New Testament (cf. the Seal of the Living God, the Rod of Jesse, the Alpha and Omega, etc.). They embrace death and life, humility and glory. The "symbolic" character of the passion and the death of the Lord consists exactly in the fact that his crucifixion is his exaltation, as he explained it himself through the "sign" of the Brazen Serpent. Nearly all the symbols of Christ further express the mystical identity between the Messias and his people. In the Old Testament, the Tree and the Mountain are symbols of the Messias, but at the same time also

of his Kingdom. In the New Testament, the vital union between the Head and the Body is even more evident. The Vine shows that the very life of the members depends on their union with Christ as the only source of salvation. The Old Testament background of the symbol of the Lamb discloses that the Lamb stands not only for the Messias, but also for the whole of the Chosen People. The Fish, the Grain, the Bread reveal the union that is established between Christ and the faithful through the Holy Eucharist. The Fish and the Pearl point out that through Baptism every individual Christian becomes another Christ, while the application of the symbol of the Fountain to Christ as well as to the Christian, shows that the selfless love of God that has saved us becomes, in us, a vital and spontaneous force breaking through the narrow limits of our selfishness and flowing freely out into others.

Like rays descending from the glorified Saviour, the symbols of Christ join together the beginning and the end of the history of redemption. They embrace death and life; they unite the Head and the members. Furthermore, they draw the whole universe into their healing power. Indeed, many of the signs of the Messias have a cosmic character. The Tree, the Mountain, the Sun, the Cornerstone, the Star in the Old Testament, the Pearl, the Grain of Wheat, the Fountain, the Door, the Lamp, the Fish in the New Testament are all deeply rooted in the common spiritual experience of mankind. The explanations of the symbols try to point out to the reader briefly the cosmic dimension proper to the signs of the Messias. A by-gone rationalistic age was all too prone to reject the symbol as being an "unscientific" approach to reality. Even in our day, many Catholics think that symbols are a "luxury" and even a dangerous one, because they so often defy definition and seem to put Christianity on an equal level with pre-Christian beliefs or superstitions. They are unaware of the power the symbol has to heal the breaches that rend the world by fitting the visible to the invisible, the material to the spiritual, the divine to the human, the individual to society. In recent years, Professor C. E. Jung and his disciples have helped us to rediscover the importance of the symbol for a fresh approach to our Christian faith; it sends its roots more deeply into the totality of the human soul than any one-sided appeal to the intellect or the will would be able to do.

More than any others will the symbols of Christ be able to heal the breaches which rend the world and souls, because they apply not only healing powers inherent in nature, but draw us into the realm of the personal sacrificial love of the Saviour, who heals the wounds of human guilt and restores an order destroyed by sin. They not only lead the stranger back into God's home, but they reveal to the Prodigal Son the face of the Father, according to the word in which Christ showed his own essence as that of a Living Symbol: "Philip, who sees me, sees the Father" (John 14:9).

The Old Testament

The Seal of the Living God

"And the Lord set a mark upon Cain, that whosoever found him should not kill him" (Gen. 4:15).

"And the Lord said: Go through the midst of Jerusalem and mark Taw upon the foreheads of the men that sigh, and mourn for all the abominations that are committed in the midst thereof" (Ezek. 9:4).

"And I saw another angel ascending from the rising of the sun, having the seal of the living God, and he cried with a loud voice to the four angels to whom it was given to harm the earth and the sea, saying: Do not harm the earth, or the sea, or the trees, till we have sealed the slaves of our God on their foreheads" (Apoc. 7:2–3).

———•••———

LONG BEFORE OUR LORD was crucified the cross was a sign sacred to men. The integrity and stability of the universe seems to rest on the cross. It points into the four directions of the compass. All living beings are shaped in the pattern of a cross. Spreading their wings in the form of a cross the birds master the air. In the power of their cruciform masts the boats cross the waves. The cross brings firmness to walls and fences and buildings. No wonder that it appeared as a sign of salvation in the earliest days of human history. It was used as a brand for animals and slaves. The illiterate used it as signature.

The last letter in the Hebrew alphabet originally was written as a so-called Greek cross with four equal arms. It was called *taw* which simply means "mark." Some of the Fathers (cf. Epistle of Barnabas 9:8; Tertullian, *Adv. Marcionem* III, 22) understood the Hebrew sign *taw* of Ezechiel 9:4 to be the *Greek* letter *taw* or the Latin T and thus were led to the conclusion that the gallows-shaped cross, the so-called *crux commissa,* was the kind of cross on which Christ died. That the Hebrew letter was written as a cross indicates that the mark on Cain's forehead and the *taw* of which Ezechiel speaks and the "seal of the Living God" of the Apocalypse, are nothing else but the cross.

The cross upon Cain's forehead is a sign of protection and mercy.[1] It saved the life of the first fratricide and made him God's own property. But it received its deepest meaning when a later and greater fratricide was committed, and Christ who had made himself one of us was crucified by us, his brothers. Since then it has become a sign of eternal life to all those who, looking at the cross, realize in true compunction of heart that they have killed their Brother. In baptism and confirmation they receive in their souls the "seal of the Living God" which is in very deed the life of the crucified and risen Lord.

"In the newly discovered world—in the darksome temple of the pagans—behold what awaits us there but the Cross of Christ!" What the Spaniards realized to their great surprise when they invaded Mexico under Cortez, is true of many other countries and nations all over the world. Rufinus reports that around the year 390 when the busts and signs of the god Serapis were removed from public places and from private houses, and the cross was painted instead on doorposts and lintels, the pagans remembered that the cross was one of their sacred signs and meant eternal life, and that their elders had told them their idols would last until the sign would appear in which there is life. Many of them, therefore, accepted the faith.[2] We meet the symbol of the cross further in the old oriental civilizations of Elam, of Sumer, in Crete and among the Germanic nations to the north.[3]

To show the esteem in which the cross was held

among the American Indians, I quote a passage from *The Sacred Pipe* (Black Elk's account of the seven rites of the Oglala Sioux): [4] "All day long the 'lamenter' sends his voice to *Wakan-Tanka* (the 'Great Spirit') for aid, and he walks as we have described upon the sacred paths which form a cross. This form has much power in it, for whenever we return to the center, we know that it is as if we are returning to *Wakan-Tanka,* who is the center of everything; and although we may think that we are going away from him, sooner or later we and all things must return to him." The cross is the sacred form that holds the world together and makes it possible for us to return to the center of all things.

A strong feeling for the stabilizing and centralizing power of the cross as a cosmological form was deeply embedded in the thinking of Greco-Roman antiquity. The World Soul, according to Plato's *Timaeus,* binds the whole world together in its breadth and length, its height and depth in the form of the *Chi* (letter written in the form of the cross). The early Greek Fathers, especially Justin and Irenaeus, interpreted these thoughts in the light of the Cross of Christ. The fact that the universe is constructed in the four dimensions of the cross and that every single thing in this visible world can only be mastered and can only subsist in the form of the cross proves to them that Jesus Christ, who at the end of time redeemed us through his Cross, is identical with the Word of God, who in the beginning created the world and sealed it with the sign of the cross for the day of redemption. The connection between the Cross of the Creator and that of the Redeemer is expressed in a classical way by Irenaeus: "He who through his obedience on the cross undid the old disobedience wrought on the tree, is himself the Word of Almighty God, permeating all of us by his invisible Presence, and, therefore, encompassing the whole world, its breadth and length, its height and depth. For through the Word of God all things are directed in their order, and the Son of God is crucified in them, because they are stamped with the form of the cross. It was right and proper that he should show in all visible things in a visible way that he is the One who illumines the heights, who reaches down into the depth, the foundations of the earth, who extends the surfaces from the Morning to the Evening, from the North to the South, who summons all that are scattered from all sides to the knowledge of the Father" (Epideixis 1:34). The Wisdom of the Word who laid the foundations of the earth reveals itself as the Wisdom of the Cross, the infinite love of Christ that St. Paul sees symbolized in the four dimensions of the cross: ". . . that being rooted and founded in charity, you may be able to comprehend, with all the saints, what is the breadth and length and height and depth: to know also the charity of Christ, which surpasseth all knowledge, that you may be filled unto all the fullness of God" (Eph. 3:17–8).

The Cross of the Redeemer is not only the recapitulation of the cosmos but also that of the Old Testament, which, as Justin says, "contains everywhere the mystery of the cross" (Dialogue 91). It is the key to the understanding of the Old Testament. "The veil in the temple was rent, that everything that was veiled in the Old Testament, should be revealed through the mystery of the Cross" (St. Augustine, *Sermo* 300:4). St. John Damascene summarizes the teachings of the Fathers on this point in *De fide orthodoxa,* IV: 11: "A prototype of the Cross was the tree of life which God had planted in paradise. . . . Jacob clearly described the cross when he blessed his sons with his arms crossed (Gen. 48:14); the staff of Moses which divided the sea, saved Israel and drowned the Egyptians (Exod. 14:6); the wood that turned the bitter waters into sweetness (Exod. 15:25); the rod with which Moses struck the rock (Exod. 17:6); the rod which gave the priesthood to Aaron (Num. 21:9); and what Moses said: 'And thy life shall be as it were hanging before thee' (Deut. 28:66) and Isaias: 'I have spread forth my hands all day to an unbelieving people' (Isa. 65:2)." Many other patterns of the cross in the Old Testament could still be added, for example, the wood of the ark that carried Noe through the flood,[5] or the ladder that Jacob saw in his dream [6] (Gen. 28:12–3), or the wood that Abraham laid on Isaac, his son, and that he then put upon the altar "in order" (Gen. 22:9), which really means "crosswise."[7]

The Tree of Life

"And the Lord brought forth of the ground all manner of trees, fair to behold and pleasant to eat of: the tree of life also in the midst of Paradise" (Gen. 2:9).

"The wisdom of God is a true tree of life to all that lay hold upon her" (Prov. 3:18).

"In the midst of the street, and on both sides of the river, was the tree of life, bearing twelve fruits, yielding its fruits every month, and the leaves of the tree were for the healing of the nations" (Apoc. 22:2).

The Old Testament

THE TREE has always played an important part in folklore and myth. It symbolizes the eternal cycle of life and death and resurrection; it is a figure as well as a pledge of community life. In spring the tree puts forth its tender buds and flowers; through the long summer its leafy branches cover both men and beasts with shade and comfort; and in fall, when its work is done and its lifegiving fruits have been plucked from its withering limbs, its sap returns to the earth for the winter to await the resurrection of spring. Families, tribes, empires are likened to trees. The cosmic tree which stands on the top of the mountain of God and upholds the dome of heaven is a symbol of world order.

The most popular survivals of the sacred tree in our days are the maypole and the Christmas tree. In spring, on the first of May, during Whitsuntide, or even on Midsummer Day, it was and still is the custom in many parts of the Old and of the New World to go out to the woods, cut down a tree and bring it into the village, where it is set up amid general rejoicings. The intention of these customs is to bring home to the village, and to each house, the blessings of the season which are embodied in the tree.[1] The blessing of the olive and palm branches on Palm Sunday gives, as it were, the Christian "fulfillment" to the old pagan custom. The olive tree is a symbol of consecration and blessing through the Spirit of God. The palm tree is the sign of victory. When the people of Jerusalem greeted the Messias (the Anointed

One) on Palm Sunday carrying palm and olive branches, they declared his triumph over death (palms) through his divine charity (olives). By taking the branches into their hands, they indicated that they were branches of the Tree of Life, the Saviour, and subjects of his kingdom. Every Palm Sunday we repeat this public adherence to the "divine policy" of Christ the King, and by taking the branches from the church into our homes, we enthrone him as the Ruler of our families, and pledge ourselves to bring God's blessing and protection over our homes by following Christ's policy: victory through charity.

The Christmas tree, in its present form, is of comparatively recent origin. It is an old medieval tradition that trees and flowers blossomed on Christmas night. But it was only after the Reformation that the Protestants, especially in northern Germany, patronized the Christmas tree to counteract the Catholic custom of having representations of the crib in the homes. It was introduced into France and England in 1840 by Princess Helena of Mecklenburg.[2]

The symbolism of a World Tree standing at the center of the earth and forming a link between the three cosmic regions of Heaven, Earth and Hell is found in ancient cultures all over the world.[3] The Oglala Sioux place a ritual image of the World Tree in the center of their sun dance lodge, which is itself considered to be an image of the universe.[4] The same meaning is attributed to the stake used in the sacrifices of Vedic India. Could the rabbinic injunction

27

that the Paschal Lamb always be roasted on a *wooden* stake (of the granate tree) have the same mythological background? [5] It is certain that the early Christians saw the relation between the stake of the Paschal Lamb and the Cross of Christ. The Cross is the Cosmic Tree, and the place where it stands, Golgotha, is the center of the world. [6] This sentence reveals the essential difference between the pagan myth and its Christian fulfillment. The pagans of all ages seek the Tree of Life within this world and with the powers of nature. The Christian Tree of Life stands on Golgotha, on "skull hill," the place where criminals suffer the death penalty for their crimes, because on this Tree of Life, the Cross, Christ heals through his obedience unto death the disobedience which our first parents had wrought at the tree in Paradise. Because his death on the Cross was the sacrifice which the Son of God offered to his Heavenly Father in loving obedience for those who through their disobedience had become God's enemies, the Christian Tree of Life is truly a way through death into Life Eternal. "Whosoever will come after me, let him deny himself and take up his cross and follow me" (Mark 8:34).

The Cross of Christ is the ladder which Jacob saw in his dream set up on the earth and the top of it reaching heaven, [7] and which St. Benedict in his Rule explained as a symbol of the Christian way of life, "on which we descend by self-exaltation and ascend by humility. [8] The whole idea of the Cross as the true Tree of Life is admirably summarized in a passage of an old homily on the Pascha of the Lord: "This Tree is my eternal salvation. It is my nourishment and my banquet. Amidst its roots I cast my own roots deep: beneath its boughs I grow and expand, reveling in its sigh as in the wind itself. Flying from the burning heat, I have pitched my tent in its shadow, and have found a resting place of dewy freshness. I flower with its flowers; its fruits bring perfect joy—fruits which have been preserved for me since time's beginning, and which now I freely eat. This Tree is a food, sweet food, for my hunger, and a fountain for my thirst; it is a clothing for my nakedness; its leaves are the breath of life. Away with the fig tree, from this time on! If I fear God, this is my protection; if I stumble, this is my support; it is the prize for which I fight and the reward of my victory. This is my straitened path, my narrow way; this is the stairway of Jacob, where angels pass up and down, and where the Lord in very truth stands at the head.

"This Tree, vast as heaven itself, rises from earth to the skies, a plant immortal, set firm in the midst of heaven and earth, base of all that is, foundation of the universe, support of this world of men, binding force of all creation, holding within itself all the mysterious essence of man. Secured with the unseen clamps of the spirit, so that, adjusted to the Divine, it may never bend or warp, with foot resting firm on earth it towers to the topmost skies, and spans with its all-embracing arms the boundless gulf of space between." [9]

29

All this symbolism of the tree has found its fulfillment in Christ. He is foreshadowed in the Tree of Life which was planted in the midst of paradise, for "the wisdom of God is a true tree of life to all that lay hold upon her" (Prov. 3:18). Christ is "the tender twig that is planted on the high mountains of Israel, that shoots forth into branches and becomes a great cedar and all the birds dwell under it" (Ezek. 17:22), whilst the "high tree," symbol of the kingdom of this world, shall be cut down (Ezek. 31:12; Dan. 4:12). Christ, who dies on the cross and rises again is indicated in the rod of Aaron (Num. 17:8) and in the dry tree which God causes to flourish (Ezek. 17:24). The risen Christ is the true vine of which we are the branches (John 15:1). He is the tree that grows on the river of the heavenly city, and yields its fruits in all eternity.

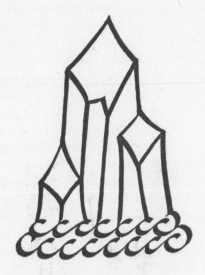

The Holy Mountain

"And in the last days the mountain of the house of the Lord shall be prepared on the top of the mountains, and it shall be exalted above the hills, and all nations shall flow unto it" (Isa. 2:2).

"A stone was cut out of the mountain without hands, and it struck the statue upon the feet . . . and broke them in pieces. . . . But the stone that struck the statue, became a great mountain, and filled the whole earth" (Dan. 2:31–35).

REMOTE AND INACCESSIBLE, rising high above this earth into the skies in lonely majesty, the mountains seem to be the natural thrones of the gods. People of old used to regard this earth as a cosmic mountain, surrounded by the waters of chaos, and surmounted by the abode of the deity. According to ideas current in the ancient East, the earth was a great hollow mountain, containing the cavernous regions of darkness—the "deep pit," the realm of the dead. The waters of the deep are kept from flooding this earth by a great rock which seals its top. Here is the entrance to the world below, the "gates of hell" (cf. Matt. 16:18). Every country is a world in miniature and has its Holy Mountain, its "navel" or link with the celestial world.[1] On the Forum in Rome we can see up to this day the place of the "omphalos" (navel) or center of the Roman Empire from which the legions set out to conquer the world. In similar fashion the Jews held that "the land of Israel is in the heart of the world, Jerusalem is in the heart of the land, the temple is in the heart of Jerusalem, and the ark of the covenant is in the midst of the temple. Next to the ark is the keystone of the world." [2]

Usually close by the central rock a well or spring flowed up from the floodwaters below, that were held back by the great rock. By the "omphalos" on the Roman Forum is Lake Juturna which the Romans believed to be the entrance to Hades. Similarly, a stream issued from the temple mount in Jerusalem. "There is a river, the streams whereof shall make glad the city of God, the holy place of the tabernacles of the most High" (Ps. 45:4). This river prefigures the waters of grace which, in the messianic times, issue forth from the Risen Lord, God's Holy Mountain of the New Covenant (Apoc. 22:1).

In Holy Scripture the history of the Holy Mountain begins with man's presumptuous attempt to build the "tower of Babel," a man-made "mountain of God" (Gen. 11). But "behold I am against thee, O destroying mountain . . . and I will stretch out my hand upon thee and roll thee down from the rocks, and will make thee a burnt mountain. And they shall not take of thee a stone for a corner" (Jer. 51:25). God's mountain is a mountain of his own choosing. He does not chose the "fat Basan" but the small and modest Mount Sion (Ps. 67:17). From this mountain the stone will be cut off which smashes the idol and grows into a mountain that fills the whole earth. The stone is Christ, who by his death and resurrection has overcome the prince of this world and has become the head of the Mystical Body which, since Pentecost, fills the whole world. The risen Christ and his Mystical Body is the "mountain of God's inheritance, the most firm habitation which God has made" (Exod. 15:17). In this mountain we are planted through baptism. But still we have to pray that we may be able "to reach that mountain which is Christ" (Feast of St. Catharine of Alexandria, *Collect*), till the other mountain "burning with fire is cast into the sea" (Apoc. 8:8).

The Old Testament

The ritual image of the Holy Mountain in our churches is the *altar*. It is usually placed on an elevated platform. In our present stone altars, three ideas are fused into one image; that of the Holy Mountain, that of the Sacred Stone, and that of the Sacred Table. The stone which forms the top of the altar is still called *mensa* (table). The Old Testament puts great emphasis on the necessity of man *building* an altar. The earth is not by itself an altar. Man has to *lift* the earth through the work of his hands. The first to build an altar was Noe when he left the ark (Gen. 8:20). In the Law of Moses, it is laid down as a rule that such an altar should not be built of hewn stone, because if any iron tool is lifted up upon it, it is polluted (Exod. 20:25). The stones of which the altar is built represent the people who build it. As long as they live in the spirit of violence, they are not fit to be the meeting place of God's mercy with the longing of his poor ones. Gideon calls the altar he erects, "Peace of the Lord" (Judg. 6:24). The altar is the place where man's willingness to follow God's will (cf. Gen. 22:9), signified in the sacrifice, meets the divine fire which descends from above to consume the human gift (III Kings 18:38), or better to transform it so that it becomes acceptable to God, and food also for men. The Hebrew word for altar, *mizbeach*, means at the same time the place of slaughter and place of meal.

From all this, it becomes evident that the altar of the New Testament is the Son of God Incarnate.

Mary built this altar by giving the human flesh. The Divine Word is the fire which descended from heaven to consume the Body of the Lord in the holocaust of the Cross, and to transform it by his Resurrection and Ascension so that it becomes "the bread of life which comes down from heaven that man may eat thereof and not die" (John 6:50). Christ himself is sacrifice and food. He is represented in the altars of our churches. "The altar is Christ," says the Roman Pontifical. The altar is the place of sacrifice, the "Golgotha" upon which Christ renews in an unbloody manner the Sacrifice of the Cross, and the altar is the table from which we receive the Bread of Life in the Sacred Banquet.

The Burning Bush

"Now Moses . . . came to the mountain of God, Horeb. And the Lord appeared to him in a flame of fire out of the midst of a bush [1]: and he saw that the bush was on fire and was not burnt. And Moses said: I will go and see this great sight, why the bush is not burnt. And the Lord called him out of the midst of the bush, and said: Moses, Moses. And he answered: Here I am. And he said: Come not nigh hither, put off the shoes from thy feet, for the place whereon thou standest is holy ground. And he said: I am the God of thy father, the God of Abraham, the God of Isaac, and the God of Jacob. . . . I am come down to de-

liver my people out of the hands of the Egyptians"
(Exod. 3:2–8).

---·---

AFTER THE FALL God made the earth bring forth
thorns which, since then, have been likened to sinners
(Gen. 3:18), good only to be set on fire and burnt to
nothing (II Kings 23:7). But when the fire of the Divine Presence descended upon the thornbush on the
Holy Mountain, the thornbush was *not* burnt. Certainly a "great sign" and full of consolation! What
else can it mean but that God will be with his people
to save them, not to judge them, although they are a
stubborn and disloyal people, and he a "devouring
fire" (Deut. 4:24).

How close the Jewish interpretation of the Burning
Bush comes to the mystery of God's saving love can be
seen from the following passage from Ginsberg, *Leg-
ends of the Jews,* Vol. II, p. 304: "God's choosing to
dwell in the stunted thornbush conveyed the knowledge to Moses that he suffers along with Israel. Furthermore Moses was taught that there is nothing in
nature, not even the insignificant and despised thornbush, that can exist without the presence of the She-
kinah (the cloud of God's glory, cf. Luke 9:34). Be-
sides, the thornbush may be taken as a symbol of
Israel in several respects. As the thornbush is the
lowliest of all the species of trees, so the condition of
Israel in exile is the lowliest as compared with that of
all other nations. . . . Further in order to give
Moses an illustration of his modesty God descended

from the exalted heaven and spake to him from a lowly thornbush instead of the summit of a lofty mountain or at the top of a stately cedar tree."

The same interpretation of the Burning Bush as a symbol of God's indwelling in the Chosen People has been given by St. Augustine. However, he understands the form of the bramble bush as referring to the sins and stubborness of the Jews, an interpretation which is much more in conformity with the general sense of the Old Testament where thorns and thistles are the sign of sin rather than of lowliness. Only with this in mind do we grasp the whole depth of meaning which Divine Wisdom was hiding under the mocking gesture of the soldiers who crowned the Lord with a crown of thorns after putting on him a scarlet robe (cf. Matt. 27:29). He was indeed the true Burning Bush, because he carried the sins of mankind in the fire of his Divine Love.

According to the Hebrew text and to the account which St. Stephen gives before the high priests (Acts 7:30) it was the "angel of the Lord" who appeared in the fire. The Fathers see in the mysterious "angel of the Lord" who so often appears in the earlier parts of the Old Testament, the Son of God, the "Angel of the great counsel" (cf. St. Augustine, *sermo* 7:3). Therefore they interpret the apparition in the burning bush as a manifestation of the Second Person of the Holy Trinity, revealing himself as the Saviour of his people. The Church adopts this interpretation when in the second of the Great Antiphons of Advent she sings: "O Adonai and Leader of the house of Israel, who appearedst in the bush to Moses in a flame of fire and gavest him the law on Sinai: come and redeem us with an outstretched arm." The sign of the Burning Bush became reality when the Word of God descended upon Mary and in her womb was united to his human nature. Christ, true God and true man, carried the "likeness of sinful flesh" (Rom. 8:3) upon the Cross that sin may be killed forever, and thus the great sign that Moses had seen in the desert was fulfilled.

However, already in early times, the Church applied the sign of the Burning Bush also to Mary, the Virgin Mother of God. On the Feast of the Circumcision, she sings: "In the bush which Moses saw was not burnt, we acknowledge the figure of thy glorious inviolate virginity: Mother of God, intercede for us." Mary herself is the picture of the Church. On Pentecost, the fire which Christ had come to cast upon the earth descended upon the apostles to burn in the bramble bush of the visible Church till New Jerusalem descends from heaven of which it is written: "The glory of God lights it up, and the Lamb is the lamp thereof" (Apoc. 21:23).

The Brazen Serpent

"And the Lord said to Moses: Make a brazen serpent and set it up for a sign: whosoever being struck shall look at it, shall live. Moses therefore made a brazen serpent, and set it up for a sign: when they that were bitten looked upon, they were healed"

(Num. 21:8–9).

"No man has ascended into heaven except him who has descended from heaven: the Son of Man who is in heaven. And as Moses lifted up the serpent in the desert, even so must the Son of Man be lifted up, that those who believe in him may not perish, but may have life everlasting" (John 3:13–15).

OF ALL THE SYMBOLS of Christ in the Old Testament the Brazen Serpent certainly is the most "shocking" one. The serpent, symbol of sin and of Satan (cf. Gen. 3:1; Apoc. 12:9), a picture of Christ! But seen in the light of the crucified Saviour the mysterious sign reveals its meaning. On the cross "He who knew no sin was made sin for us, so that in him we might be made the justice of God" (II Cor. 5:21). Not a real serpent, but the brazen *likeness* of it was lifted up in the desert. So did Christ come in the *likeness* of sinful flesh (Rom. 8:3), taking upon himself the pains of sin, without sin (Heb. 4:15). As the serpent was lifted up on the pole, so he was lifted up on the cross, and as the likeness of the serpent was made of metal as a lasting memorial, so did the death of the Saviour become a lasting memorial in the Holy Sacrifice of the Mass.

All those who are bitten by the serpents of their sins should turn to the crucified Saviour, to be healed from their wounds. Only one condition do they have to fulfill. The Book of Wisdom points to it: "He that turned to the Brazen Serpent was not healed by that which he saw, but by thee the Saviour of all. . . . For it is thou, O Lord, that hast power of life and death, and leadest down to the gates of death and bringest back again" (Wisd. 16:7, 13). Only those, who, looking at the crucified Saviour, say with the centurion under the cross: "Truly this man was the Son of God," will receive new and everlasting life.

Nobody has explained the meaning of the Brazen Serpent in a more vivid manner than St. Augustine in the twelfth sermon on the Gospel of St. John: "In this was shown a great mystery, the figure of a thing to come. . . . What are the biting serpents? Sins from the mortality of the flesh. What is the serpent lifted up? The Lord's death on the cross. For as death came by the serpent, it was figured by the image of a serpent. The serpent's bite was deadly, the Lord's death is life-giving. A serpent is gazed on, that the serpent may have no power. What is this? A death is gazed on, that death may have no power. But whose death? The death of life. . . . Is not Christ the life? And yet Christ hung on the cross. Is not Christ life? And yet Christ was dead. But in Christ's death, death died. Life dead, slew death; the fullness of life swallowed up death; death was absorbed in the body of Christ. So also shall we say in the resurrection when now triumphant we shall sing: 'Where, O death, is thy victory? Where, O death, is thy sting?' Meanwhile, brethren, that we may be healed from sin, let us now gaze on Christ crucified. . . . Just as they who looked on that serpent perished not by the serpent's bites, so they who look in faith on Christ's death are healed from the bites of sin. But those were healed from death to temporal life; whilst here he says: 'that they may have everlasting life.' Now there is this difference between the figurative image and the real thing: the figure procured temporal life; the reality, of which that was the figure, procures eternal life."

The Star of Jacob

"Balaam the son of Beor, the man whose eyes are open, has said: I shall see him, but not now: I shall behold him, but not nigh: there shall come a star out of Jacob, and a sceptre shall rise out of Israel, and shall strike the chiefs of Moab" (Num. 24:17).

"Now when Jesus was born in Bethlehem of Juda in the days of Herod the king, behold there came wise men from the east to Jerusalem, saying, where is he that is born king of the Jews? for we have seen his star in the east, and are come to adore him" (Matt. 2:2).

"I, Jesus, am the bright morning star" (Apoc. 22:16).

———◦•◦———

THE FACT that the course of the celestial bodies in-
fluences life on earth led people of old to the belief
that the heavenly world of the stars is the archetype
and model of the earthly world, and that the stars in
their unchangeable course—*dei aeterni,* as the
Greeks used to call them—determine the fate of man.

In the Old Testament the stars are not gods. They
are the obedient servants of the Lord of hosts who
created them. "They were called and they said: Here
we are: and with cheerfulness they have shined forth
to him that made them" (Baruch 3:35). When God
laid the cornerstone of the earth, "the morning stars
sang together, and all the sons of God shouted with
joy" (Job 38:7). The stars are symbols of the just who
obey God's commands and, therefore, declare his glory.

The king of Babylon is the rebellious star who
wants to rule without serving his God. He is over-
thrown by the creator of heaven and earth, as Isaias
says of him: "How art thou fallen from heaven, Lucifer, son of the morning? How art thou fallen to the
earth that didst wound the nations?" (Isa. 14:12).
Only one star will rise to world domination: the "Star
of Jacob," the Messias. He is the "morning star," because he was begotten before the day of creation (Ps.
109).

When he appears here on earth, he rises in the dark
of night like the morning star; at his birth in the
stable of Bethlehem, at his Resurrection from the

dead, at his Second Coming. Each one of these three risings is announced by a star. The royal star leads the magi to the crib of the newborn King of the Jews (Matt. 2:2–9). The morning star which rises victoriously out of the Easter night and greets the Saviour at the dawn of the Resurrection is praised by the deacon in the *Exsultet* of the Paschal vigil: "May the morning star find the flame of this candle alive; that Lucifer who knows no setting, that Star who, returning from hell, shone serenely upon mankind." When the end of darkness has come and the last day dawns, the true Lucifer reveals himself saying: "I am the bright and morning star." (Apoc. 22:16)

In perfect obedience to his Heavenly Father, the star of Christ has run its course. His death on the Cross was his setting as the evening star. His Resurrection was his rising as the morning star. All those who die with him and rise with him in baptism and open themselves to his light have become "sons of the morning star, sons of God" (St. Jerome, *In Job* 38). When the last day dawns, the day star will arise in their hearts (cf. II Peter 1:19), and they will hear from the lips of the Risen Saviour the blessed words: "I will give you the morning star." (Apoc. 2:28)

Again let us listen to the inspired words of the same preacher who has already announced to us the glories of the Tree of Life: "Behold the hallowed rays of the light of Christ are shining. The pure flames of the pure Spirit are rising. The heavenly treasures of glory and divinity have been opened. The night, immense and dark, has been swallowed up. The dismal gloom of darkness has been dispelled by this new light, and the sad shadow of death has vanished. Life radiates over the entire realm of being, and everything is filled with light. The morning of mornings rules the universe, and he who was before the morning star and before all the lights, the immortal and infinite, the great Christ, blazes more brightly than the sun. This is why to all of us who believe in him a day of light has risen, the eternal day that knows no end, the mystical Pascha, the great and wonderful Pascha, the masterpiece of divine omnipotence, the true feast, the eternal memorial: immortality rising out of death, life emerging from the tomb, healing stemming from suffering, resurrection resulting from the fall, Ascension following the Descent. This is the way in which God works his great deeds. Through the impossible he creates the unbelievable, that we may know that he alone accomplishes all he wills." [1]

The Rod of Jesse

"And there shall come forth a rod out of the root of Jesse, and a flower shall rise up out of his root. And the spirit of the Lord shall rest upon him" (Isa. 11:1).

"Behold the days come, saith the Lord, and I will raise unto David a righteous branch, and a king shall reign and prosper, and shall execute justice and judgment in the earth" (Jer. 23:5).

"Behold the man whose name is "the Offspring," and he shall grow up out of this place and he shall build the temple of the Lord" (Zach. 6:12).

"I, Jesus, am the root and the offspring of David" (Apoc. 22:16).

———•◆•———

ONE OF THE TITLES that was used for the king in the ancient East was that of the "Branch" or the "Offspring." It designates the king as the legitimate ruler, the scion of an old family which traces its origins back to the gods.

The Old Testament lives in the expectation of the "Offspring," the Messias, whom God had promised solemnly to David: "I will raise up thy seed after thee . . . and I will establish the throne of his kingdom forever. I will be to him a father, and he shall be to me a son" (II Kings 7). This promise became true when Jesus was born of the seed of David according to the flesh (Rom. 1, 3). He was truly the Son of his Heavenly Father from all eternity. His throne was established forever when God raised him up from the dead, not to return any more to corruption (Acts 13, 34).

This Jesus is the "Rod of Jesse." The full meaning of this expression becomes clearer when we go back to the Hebrew text of the entire passage: "And there shall come forth a *shoot* from the *stump* of Jesse, and a *sapling* from its roots shall *bear fruit*" (Isa. 11:1). The emphasis of the text is evidently on the difference between humble beginnings and a glorious end. The shoot comes forth from the "stump of Jesse." The tree which represents the house of David will have shared the fate of the other trees of the forest (the Jewish people), and be reduced to a charred stump, to the original lowliness of Jesse's family in Bethlehem, when the Saviour is born from it, like a *shoot* which promises to replace the bole and the top of the Davidic tree. He is first only a tender little bud or sapling (in Hebrew, *nezer*). The very sound of this word echoes in the report which St. Matthew gives of the fulfillment of this prophecy: "He will be called a 'Nazarene.' " (Matt. 2:23).[1] But from this humble beginning, the Messianic sapling will develop into a tree bearing much fruit (cf. Ezek. 17:23). Through his Resurrection he becomes the "Lord of the Spirit" (II Corinthians 3:18), the flower which breathes the "sweet odor of Christ," the Holy Spirit, into the hearts of the faithful, the fruit which they pick from the Tree of Life of the Risen Saviour in Holy Communion.

In the course of the Paschal vigil, the Church reads still another prophecy of Isaias which is apt to lead us more deeply into the mystery of the "Rod of Jesse": "In that day the *offspring of the Lord* shall be in magnificence and glory, and the *fruit of the earth* shall be high, and a great joy to them that have survived of Israel" (Isa. 4:2). "That day" is the day of the Messias. He is called, "offspring of the Lord" (cf. Jer. 23:5, 33:15; Zach. 3:8, 6:12). The Hebrew *zemach* has been rendered by the Greek *anatole* and the Latin *oriens,* both with the meaning of "dayspring." Thus the "Offspring of the Lord" becomes the "Dayspring from on high" in the song of Zachary (Luke 1:78). Both of these terms point to the divine origin of the Messias as Son of God, while the other name, "Fruit of the earth," indicates his human origin from the Virgin Mary.

In his commentary on Isaias, St. Jerome mentions the change of interpretation to which the Vulgate translation of Isaias 11:1 has given rise. This version reads: "There shall come forth a *stem* out of the root of Jesse, and a *flower* shall rise out of his *root.*" It is interpreted by St. Ambrose in the following manner: "The root is the family of the Jews, the stem is Mary, the flower of Mary is Christ" (*De benedictionibus Patriarcharum,* n. 19). From here, it was only one step to apply the "root of Jesse" to Our Lady, as it is done in the antiphon which accompanies us through Lent: "Queen of the heavens, we hail thee. . . . Thou the root, thou the door, whence the world's true light is risen."

The messianic interpretation of the symbolism of the Rod of Jesse is kept in the third of the Great Antiphons in Advent: "O Root of Jesse, who standest for an ensign of the people, before whom kings shall keep silence, and unto whom the Gentiles shall make their supplications: come to deliver us and tarry not." The text recalls Isaias 11:10. "And it shall come to pass in that day that the root of Jesse, standing, shall be as an ensign to the nations. Unto it shall the nations appeal, and its abiding place shall be glorious." Here the Messias is identified with the root out of which he is risen. He appears on his day in the glory of his royal power, like a scepter which rules and unites the nations, and takes his place in heavenly glory at the right hand of his Father. He is "the lion of the tribe of Juda, the root of David, who has prevailed to open the book" (Apoc. 5:5). He reveals himself in a sentence containing the whole meaning of the symbolism of the Rod of Jesse: "I am the root and the offspring of David, the bright and morning star" (Apoc. 22:16).

The Key of David

"And the key of the house of David will I lay upon his shoulder: and he shall open and none shall shut: and he shall shut, and none shall open" (Isa. 22:22).

"And I will give to thee the keys of the kingdom of heaven. And whatsoever thou shalt bind upon earth, it shall be bound also in heaven: and whatsoever thou shalt loose on earth, it shall be loosed also in heaven" (Matt. 16:19).

"Thus says the holy one, the true one, he who has the key of David, he who opens and no one shuts, and who shuts and no one opens" (Apoc. 3:7).

HE WHO HOLDS the keys of the house wields power over it. When a city surrenders, the keys are brought to the conqueror, not only the keys of the gates, but also the keys of the storehouse and those of the prison house as well.

The "power of the keys" is threefold: over the entrance gate to admit or to exclude, over the prison to punish or to condone, over the storehouse and the treasure to feed and to reward.

Isaias tells us (22:22) how Eljakim received the "key of the house of David" and, thence, received full power over the royal palace and the whole kingdom as administrator and representative of the king.

Eljakim is an archetype of the Messias, the "offspring of David," to whom is given, at the end of time, full power over the messianic kingdom which was promised to the house of David. The glorified and exalted Christ has received from his Heavenly Father the "key of David" (Apoc. 3:7) with its threefold power. Through his death he has conquered death and possesses "the keys of death and of Hades" (Apoc. 1:18) to "bring the prisoners out of the prison house, them that sit in darkness and in the shadow of death" (O Antiphon). He has power over the gates of the heavenly Jerusalem. All its citizens are written in the "book of life of the Lamb" (Apoc. 21:27). Finally the risen Christ has the key to the heavenly storehouse, for, as St. Peter says (Acts 2:23), "exalted by the right hand of God, and receiving from the Father the promise of the Holy Spirit, he has poured forth this Spirit which you see and hear."

At Cesarea Philippi, Christ gave the "power of the keys" to St. Peter: "And I will give to thee the keys of the kingdom of heaven. And whatever thou shalt bind upon earth, it shall be bound also in heaven: and whatever thou shalt loose on earth, it shall be loosed in heaven" (Matt. 16:19). The study of biblical and late Jewish language and custom gives ample proof that the handing over of the keys signifies true delegation of authority. With his words, Our Lord does not promise St. Peter that he will one time be the "porter of heaven," but he invests him here and now with the power symbolized by the keys to govern the Church spiritually, which is threefold: the power of teaching, the "key of knowledge" (Luke 11:52); the power of administering the spiritual wealth of the Church through the sacraments; and the power of judgment or jurisdiction.[1]

The fact that Christ delegated his authority to St. Peter and the other Apostles (John 20:23) keeps him present in the Church as the Key to whom she addresses herself in the fourth of the Great Antiphons of Advent: "O Key of David, and Scepter of the house of Israel, who openest and no man shutteth, who shuttest and no man openeth: come and bring forth from his prison house the captive that sitteth in darkness and in the shadow of death."

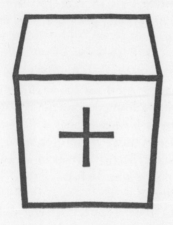

The Cornerstone

"The stone which the builders rejected, has become the head of the corner. This is the Lord's doing: and it is wonderful in our eyes" (Ps. 117:22–23).

"And Jesus said: What then is this that is written: The stone which the builders rejected, has become the cornerstone? Everyone who falls upon that stone will be broken to pieces, but upon whomever it falls, it will grind him to powder" (Luke 20:17–18).

"You are built upon the foundations of the apostles and the prophets with Christ Jesus himself as the chief cornerstone . . . in him you are being built together into a dwelling place for God in the Spirit" (Eph. 2:20–22).

STONE IS FIRM and lasting. Builders test their stones selecting the most solid for foundations on which to rear the whole building, for cornerstones to hold the walls together, or for headstones which will lock into a single mass the entire structure. Stone likewise offers firm resistance to the thrusts of an enemy; it will crush him upon whom it falls; it will bruise those who fall against it.

God is the "stone of Israel" (Gen. 49:24), because he is a God of truth and his mercies endure forever. His faithfulness towards his people is the firm and precious cornerstone which is laid in Sion (Isa. 28:16). In Christ Jesus, God's loyalty becomes manifest. He is the stone that the leaders of Israel rejected when they crucified him that was chosen by God, however, to become the cornerstone when he rose from the dead (cf. Acts 4:10–1). When we try to penetrate into the meaning of the symbolism of the cornerstone, we discover that various ideas are fused in this picture. The idea of the *foundation stone* is clearly expressed in Isaias 28:16: "Thus saith the Lord God: Behold I lay in Zion for a foundation a stone, a tried stone, a precious cornerstone, a sure foundation: he that believeth shall not make haste." Christ is the foundation stone, "for other foundation no man can lay but that which is laid, which is Christ Jesus" (I Cor. 3:11). He

alone has wrought our redemption by dying for us
and rising for us. We depend entirely on his work and
on his strength. The Hebrew word used in Psalm
117:22, *rosch pinnah*—still surviving in our word
"pinnacle"—has been translated in various ways as
"head of the corner," "cornerstone," or "headstone."
The idea of the cornerstone implies that Christ is
a part of the foundation, but its most important, visible part, the part which binds the walls. This is true
of Christ, because in him the two walls of God and
mankind, of the Jews and the Gentiles, of the Old
and the New Testament meet. It is in this sense that
the Church sings in the sixth of the Great Antiphons
of Advent: "O King of the Gentiles, and the Desired
of them, *Thou cornerstone that makest both one:*
come and deliver man whom Thou didst form out of
the dust of the earth." In the beautiful hymn we sing
on the feast of the dedication of a church, both
meanings, that of the foundation and that of the cornerstone, are combined into one:

> Christ is made the sure foundation,
> And the Precious Cornerstone
> Who, the two walls underlying,
> Bound in each, binds both in one,
> Holy Sion's help forever,
> And her confidence alone.

In recent years, more and more scholars agree with an
opinion first proposed by Joachim Jeremias [1] that
rosch pinnah is rather the *headstone,* or capstone,

which holds a vault or an arch together.[2] The Risen Saviour is indeed the headstone of the spiritual temple in which the whole building culminates, which holds it together and defines its design (Eph. 2:20; Zach. 4:7). This threefold meaning of Christ as the cornerstone is well expressed by Cynewulf in his poem "Christ." Interpreting the Great Antiphon which has previously been quoted, he says:

> Thou art the wall stone
> That the workers once threw out from the work,
> Well it becomes Thee that Thou be head
> Of a mighty hall and weld together
> Its wide walls in fast union,
> Flint unbreakable, that throughout earth's dwelling
> All that have eyes may wonder evermore,
> O Lord of Glory.

While Christ, as a cornerstone, holds the structure of the faithful together as a living Temple, he becomes a "stone of stumbling and a rock of offence" (cf. Isa. 8:14; I Pet. 2:8), to all those who do not believe in him. On the Day of Judgment, the stone will fall down from the mountain (Luke 20:18) to smash the idols of men and will grow into a rock "higher than the hills, foursquare, so that it could hold the whole world." [3]

The Sun of Justice

"For behold the day shall come kindled as a furnace: and all the proud, and all that do wickedly shall be stubble: and the day that comes shall set them on fire. . . . But unto you that fear my name, the Sun of Justice shall arise, and health in his wings" (Mal. 4:1–2).

"And after six days Jesus takes Peter, James and John his brother and brings them up into a high mountain apart: and he was transfigured before them: and his face did shine as the sun" (Matt. 17:1–2).

"And I saw one . . . like to the Son of Man . . . and his countenance was as the sun shining in its power" (Apoc. 1:16).

————•—•—•————

IN ANTIQUITY, when our concept of "nature" as regulated by "laws" was unknown, the sun, the moon and the stars were regarded as "powers." The sun appeared to be a mighty ruler who every morning conquers the powers of darkness and "rejoices as a giant to run the way" (Ps. 18). From the height of the skies it gives light and life to the world, and "there is no one that can hide himself from his heat" (Ps. 18). The sun was conqueror, ruler and judge.

Christ is "the Sun of Justice." [1] He is God's eternal Wisdom, "the brightness of eternal light and the unspotted mirror of God's majesty" (Wis. 7:26). His crucifixion is likened to the setting of the sun. He descended into "the lower parts of the earth" (Eph. 4:9) to bring light to those who were waiting in darkness and in the shadow of death. In his Resurrection he became "the dayspring from on high" (Luke 1:79), the bringer of a new age of light, of life and of salvation to his Church which is likened to the moon, receiving its light from the sun. The whole life of the Church and of Christians is turned toward Christ as to the sun. The first day of the week, the "Sunday," is celebrated as the weekly memorial of Christ's Resurrection. Churches and altars look in the direction of the rising sun. At Baptism the Sun of Justice illumines the hearts of the neophytes so that they sing,

together with all Christians: "As the sun is the joy of
those who seek the day, so is the Lord my joy because
he is my sun" (Odes of Solomon); and every Monday
when the Church greets the rising sun at the hour of
Lauds, she sings:

> Thou brightness of the Father's ray,
> True Light of Light and Day of Day,
> Light's Fountain and Eternal Spring,
> Thou Morn the morn illumining!
> Glide in, Thou very Sun Divine,
> With everlasting brightness shine:
> And shed abroad in every sense
> The Spirit's light and influence.

The New Testament

The Lamb of God

————•◦•————

"He was offered, because it was his own will, and he opened not his mouth: he shall be led as a sheep to the slaughter, and shall be dumb as a lamb before the shearer, and he shall not open his mouth" (Isa. 53:7).

"The next day John saw Jesus coming towards him, and he said: Behold the Lamb of God, who takes away the sin of the world!" (John 1:29).

"And I saw: and behold, in the midst of the throne, and of the four living creatures, and in the midst of

65

the elders, a Lamb standing, as if slain . . ." (Apoc. 5:6).

———————•◆•◆•———————

THE LAMB is innocent, gentle, guileless. It puts complete trust in the shepherd, whose voice it knows, and whom it follows in meek obedience. When led to the slaughter it opens not its mouth, but confidently walks where it is led.

In Old Covenant times, God, the Good Shepherd, chose Israel as his beloved lamb. It listened to his voice on Mount Sinai and followed him through the desert to the pastures of the Promised Land. The lamb, therefore, became the symbol of the Israelitic people. Enjoying God's love and care Israel sings the "canticle of the lamb": "The Lord is my shepherd, I shall not want" (Ps. 22). In need and distress Israel cries to the Shepherd: "Thou hast given us like sheep to be eaten . . . for thy sake we are counted as sheep for the slaughter" (Ps. 43).

Also in the Paschal Lamb the Jews see a symbol of the Chosen People, as appears from the following legend: "Pharao had a dream. Seated on his royal throne he lifted up his eyes and saw before him an elder setting up before the king a shopkeeper's scales. The old man took all the mighty ones of Egypt, her princes, her warriors and all their armor, and placed them on one pan of the balance. On the other he put a single little lamb. And behold the little lamb turned the scales! Pharao was astounded at this vision, of a suckling lamb outweighing all the mighty

ones of Egypt" (Sefer-Ha-yashar 128a). Israel weighed
heavier than all the power of Egypt because it was
God's first-born child—the one upon whom his loving
eyes rested.

Why was it, then, that only the blood of the lamb
was able to save Israel in Egypt, and that every morning and evening a lamb had to be offered for the sins
of the people (Exod. 29, 39)? Why should the very
object of God's love be offered as a sacrifice for the
sins of the many? The reason for this remains hidden
to the eyes of the Jews. Israel's sufferings raise in
them the question: "Why is thy wrath enkindled
against the sheep of thy pasture" (Ps. 73:1)? Only
the prophet Isaias brings light into the darkness of
this mystery: "All we like sheep have gone astray
. . . and the Lord has laid on him the guilt of us
all. . . . He shall be led as a sheep to the slaughter"
Isa. 53). When the sheep had strayed, and had gone
each his own way, one would come, the *true* Lamb,
the *true* Israel. In him the many sheep are con-
tracted, as it were, into one, who is the substance of
all Israel. He is God's Son who descended from
heaven, and by becoming the Son of David, was
made the Lamb of God. Innocent in his divine
splendor, gentle in his human lowliness, guileless, as
befits the *Truth*, he opened not his mouth when led
to the slaughter. On Calvary, he was sacrificed as the
true Lamb of God, because the Innocent took upon
himself the sins of the many.

The Shepherd became the Lamb. In the parable of

the lost sheep (Matt. 18:12; Luke 15:4), the shepherd is the Word of God who leaves the ninety-nine sheep, the angels, on the mountains of heaven, and descends into the valley of this world to seek after the lamb that was lost when Adam fell. He finds it when in the womb of Mary he becomes man. He takes it upon his shoulders in his death on the Cross. He brings it back into the fold in his glorious ascension.[1] Christ is shepherd and lamb in one, as Jacob was (Gen. 48:15). He is shepherd as the Word of God, the *logos* whom Philon of Alexandria calls "shepherd of the universe." He is shepherd also because he is anointed with the Spirit, and, therefore, able to lead his flock to the waters of life.[2]

After his victory, seated on God's throne, the Lamb, as the Shepherd, guides the new flock unto the fountains of the waters of life (Apoc. 7:16). His lambs are those who listen to his voice in faith, drink the clear waters of the Spirit from the fountains of Baptism, and feed on the pasture of the Eucharist. During their earthly life they are "reckoned no better than sheep marked down for the slaughter" (Rom. 8:36), till the final triumph of the Lamb. Then, skipping over the hills of eternity, they will sing the new song of the Lamb.

The Door

* • *

"Amen, amen, I say to you, he who enters not by the door into the sheepfold, but climbs up another way, is a thief and a robber. But he who enters by the door is the shepherd of the sheep. . . . Amen, amen, I say to you, I am the door of the sheep. Those others who have come are thieves and robbers. I am the door. . . . If anyone enter by me he shall find salvation, and shall go in and out, and shall find pastures" (John 10:1, 2, 7, 8, 9).

* • *

To PASS through a door is an *initiation* and a *consecration,* because it means to leave behind the past and to enter into a new life. To the Romans of old, the victorious army, by marching through the arch of triumph, was cleansed of past offenses and consecrated to a new era of peace. For the people of the Old Testament, the temple gate of Jerusalem took the place of the arch of triumph. No armies marched through it, but the festive throngs of the pilgrims approached it in solemn procession on the Feast of the Tabernacles. Their summons rang out to the warders: "This is the gate of the Lord. The righteous shall enter into it!" (Ps. 117:19–20).

The real door to the Messianic era, however, is not made of stone. It is the living heart of the Saviour. The very shape of the door indicates salvation through Christ, because its two sideposts, holding up the lintel, form a gallows-shaped cross. Every wall effects a separation between those within, whom it protects, and those without, whom it excludes. Walls, therefore, are needed only in a world where enmity exists between those who share in the blessedness of a common life and those who are strangers and exiles. The door, however, pierces the wall, and unites the two groups—in the power of the cross.

After the earth had been cursed, and enmity placed between the serpent and the woman, Paradise was walled off from the rest of the world. But the gate remained, guarded by the cherub with the flaming sword—waiting for the time of man's re-entrance. God also hid his Holy Presence behind the walls of the temple, but a door remained, through which, once a year, the high priest was allowed to enter the Holy of Holies.

When Christ extended his hands on the Cross he became the Door through which the wall of separation between God and man was opened. The cherub at the gate of Paradise put away his sword when God's Eternal Love, hanging on the Cross, said to the good thief: "This day you shall be with me in Paradise!" When Christ gave up the ghost, the curtain of the Holy of Holies was rent, to indicate that we can "enter the sanctuary through the blood of Jesus" (Heb. 10:19). Christ is the Door through which we have access to the Father, because he is the sacrificial victim which reconciles us in one body to God, so that we are citizens with the saints and members of God's household (cf. Eph. 2:16 ff.).

This Door was foreshadowed in the door of Noe's ark, which, significantly enough, "was set in the side thereof" (Gen. 6:16); the Door was opened when the lance of the soldier pierced the side of Jesus (John 19:34). We enter through this Door by being baptized into the Death and Resurrection of Christ, through which we are cleansed from past offenses and consecrated as children of the Heavenly Father.

The Christian symbolism of the Door found its most beautiful expression in the mighty portals of medieval cathedrals. They are the holy gates through which the faithful enter into the joy of the Lord. In some of them, as for example in Amiens, the glorified Christ holds the central place. His Resurrection, his

Ascension, or his glorious Second Coming may be represented. In others, we find the five prudent virgins on one side and the five foolish ones on the other to remind the faithful that their entering into this earthly church is a foreshadowing of their final entering into the door of Christ's wedding hall, to which we should not come late. In others again, the visitor finds himself surrounded with scenes from the life of Mary. She is the door "through which no man has passed" (Ezek. 44:2).

The Lamp

"Command the children of Israel that they bring the purest oil of crushed olives for the lights, that a lamp may burn from evening until morning in the tent of meeting" (Exod. 27:20).

"For Sion's sake I will not keep silent, and for Jerusalem's sake I will not rest till her Just One come forth as brightness, and her Saviour be lighted as a lamp" Isa. 62:1).

"I am the light of the world" (John 8:12).

73

"You were once darkness, but now you are light in the Lord. Walk then as children of light" (Eph. 5:8).

"And the City had no need of the sun, neither of the moon to shine in it: for the glory of God lights it up, and the Lamb is the lamp thereof" (Apoc. 21:23–24).

———◦•◦•◦———

THE SYMBOL of the burning lamp appears in the history of our salvation for the first time in Abraham's vision (Gen. 15:12–17), when at sunset a trance came upon him and a great and gloomy terror seized upon him, and he saw, in the thick darkness, a smoking furnace and a burning torch passing between the pieces of the sacrifice. In this vision, the ancestor of Israel anticipated the whole history of his people, especially their sufferings in Egypt and their liberation. The burning torch refers to the "pillar of fire" which, during the night, showed the Chosen People the way out of Egypt into the land of promise and of true liberty (Exod. 13:21). It points further to the first Good Friday when the Paschal Lamb of the New Testament was offered on the Cross, and night covered the earth, and the burning torch of Christ's undying sacrificial love opened to the New Israel the way out of the slavery of sin into freedom of the Spirit.

God commanded that a lamp should burn throughout the night in the tent of meeting, before the veil of the Holy of Holies, and he showed the pattern of the candlestick to Moses on the mount. It was to be

made of pure gold, shaped like an almond tree, the
first tree to bloom in spring, with three branches on
either side of the central stem, decorated with almond
blossoms, supporting seven cups for seven lamps. Life,
which he raises from death, and light, which he calls
out of darkness, are the great gifts which God in his
infinite mercy bestows upon the Chosen People, that
he may make of them "the lamp of the nations" (Isa.
42:6).

The picture of the seven-branched candlestick un-
derlies the prophecy in which Isaias sees the sevenfold
Spirit of the Lord descending upon the Rod of Jesse.
It refers first to David, who is anointed with the
Spirit. He is the lamp of Israel (II Kings 21:17) which
will be kept burning in Jerusalem (III Kings 11:36;
IV Kings 8:19) through his successors. However, only
the Risen Messias, who shines in the fire of the sevenfold Spirit, fulfills the divine pledge: "I have prepared a lamp for my anointed" (Ps. 131:17).

The lamp in the sanctuary was a promise of the
fullness of the sevenfold Spirit, which descended upon
the shoot of the stem of Jesse, Jesus Christ, the Son of
David. He is the Lamp, because he is the Lamb whose
sacrificial love, burning like a torch on the Cross, has
expelled the darkness of death, and has become the
lamp of the New Jerusalem (Apoc. 21:23). He is the
Lamp, because, exalted into heaven, he has been
anointed with the fullness of the Spirit, and has become the golden candlestick which Zachary the
prophet saw, and which the angel told him held "the

seven eyes of the Lord which range over the whole earth" (Zach. 4:3–10).

In the Easter night the light of the Risen Christ is brought into the dark church. The burning Easter candle is dipped into the baptismal font, and out of it the faithful are born as "children of the light" (I Thess. 5:4–5). By loving one another they let their light shine before men (Matt. 5:14–16), and, like the prudent virgins, they keep their lamps burning until the bridegroom comes (Matt. 25:1–13).

The Fountain of Life

"Then you shall draw water with joy from the wells of the Saviour" (Isa. 12:3).

"On the last, the greatest day of the feast, Jesus stood there and cried aloud: 'If any man thirst, let him come to me and drink. He who believes in me, as the Scripture says, "rivers of living water shall flow from his bosom."' He said this, however, of the Spirit whom they who believed in him were to receive" (John 7:37–39).

"When they came to Jesus and saw that he was already dead, they did not break his legs; but one of the soldiers opened his side with a lance, and immediately blood and water flowed out" (John 19:33–34).

———•—•—•———

ONLY PEOPLE who dwell in a desert country can appreciate the blessing of a spring. In the Near East, the common name for "spring" is "God's gift" (cf. John 4:10). This name applies only to the fountain of *living* water, but never to the man-made cistern, wherefore the prophet says: "They have forsaken me, the Fountain of living water, to hew for themselves cisterns, broken cisterns that can hold no water" (Jer. 2:13).

Crystal clear, exuberant, ever renewing itself, the fountain wells up from the deep. With friendly murmur it cheers the weary pilgrim. Freely it spends itself to quench his thirst, and to cleanse his dust-covered face. The spring talks, cleanses, and refreshes. This threefold function of the spring is a wonderful symbol of the mission of Our Saviour. Therefore, the prophet sees in the fountain a symbol of the coming Messias as he exclaims: "Then you shall draw water with joy from the springs of the Saviour!" The Messias is the Word of God, the "Fountain of Wisdom" (Eccles. 1:5). He preaches the glad tidings of the approaching Kingdom of God to those who "have ears to hear." He comes to spend himself, to cleanse us with his Blood, to refresh us with his Spirit.

This fountain was foreshadowed in the river which watered the garden of Eden, and separated into four branches, as the life-giving voice of Christ has been divided into the four gospels, to reach unto the whole earth. Again, the "spiritual rock," which gave water to the thirsting people of God in the desert, was Christ (I Cor. 10–4). One day, when the Jews were celebrating the Feast of the Tabernacles, in memory of Israel's sojourn in the desert, and they poured out water at the foot of the altar, in commemoration of the rock and the fountain, Jesus stood in the midst of them, and cried aloud: "If any man thirst, let him come to me, and drink!" (John 7:37). Indeed, the crucified Wisdom of God poured out rivers of life. When the soldier opened his side with a lance, blood and water gushed forth. The tomb in the rock became the fountain of the Resurrection. The glorified Lord poured out his Spirit over the Church on Pentecost.

To those who receive it, the water of the Spirit turns into a spring welling up unto eternal life [1] (John 4:14). Extinguishing in the reborn Christian the fires of self-love, it overcomes in him the "law of gravitation" proper to the flesh. With St. Ignatius of Antioch (Rom. 7:2) he says: "My 'eros' has been crucified, and there is in me no fire of love for earthly things, but only water living and speaking in me and saying to me from within: 'Come to the Father.' "

The True Vine

"I am the true vine, and my Father is the vinedresser. Every branch in me that bears no fruit he cuts away; and every branch that bears fruit he trims clean, that it may bear more fruit. You are already clean because of the word that I have spoken to you. Remain in me and I in you. As the branch cannot bear fruit of itself unless it remain in the vine, so neither can you, unless you remain in me. I am the vine, you are the branches. He who remains in me and I in him, he bears much fruit; for without me you can do nothing. If anyone does not remain in me, he can only be like the branch that is cast off and withers away. Such a branch is

picked up and thrown into the fire to burn there"
(John 15:1–6).

————•◦•————

THE VINE has many shoots, which rapidly run wild if
left without proper care. But if these are pruned and
trimmed, they yield fruit in abundance. In Oriental
mythology, the vine was considered as the Tree of
Life, in opposition to the fig tree, the tree of death.[1]
Noe planted the vine on the new earth which had
been cleansed by the waters of the Flood (Gen. 9:20).
The writers of the Old Testament saw in the vine a
fitting symbol of God's Chosen People. God planted
this vine in the Promised Land. There it took root,
spread rapidly, and filled the land (Ps. 79:9–12). In
the end, however, the Divine Husbandman was dis-
appointed in his vine: "I planted you a choice vine,
all true seed; how then are you changed to a rank
vine, a wild plant?" (Jer. 2:21).

Only Our Lord Jesus Christ could say of himself:
"I am the true vine," because he was the Son of God,
who assumed flesh that fleshly men might be grafted
as branches into him, the Vine. Christ could not have
been the Vine except he became man, yet he could
not have instilled divine life into the branches had
he not been God.[2]

By being planted into his Death and Resurrection
in Baptism, and nourished by the body of the Risen
Saviour in the Holy Eucharist, we live in an organic
union with Christ. As the branches derive all their
vigor and sap from the vine, so do we bear fruit, not

of ourselves, but through the grace of Christ. "For since Christ Jesus is himself the Head to the members, and as the Vine to the branches, he causes virtue (i.e., spiritual life) continually to flow into them, which virtue always precedes their good works, accompanies and follows them, and without it they are not able in any manner to be pleasing to God and meritorious." [3] The branches which do not draw their strength from the Vine are doomed to wither. They must be cut away: they are good for nothing but firewood. The good branches must be pruned—the pruning knife is the "word" which Christ spoke, that is, his passion and death (cf. John 15:3).

The True Vine, therefore, symbolizes Jesus, the God-Man, our union with him and our dependence on him. It declares God's punishment of those who separate from him, and his blessing on those who abide in him.

The Grain of Wheat

"The hour has come now for the Son of Man to be glorified. Amen, amen, I say unto you: unless the grain of wheat fall unto the ground and die, it remains alone. But if it die, it brings forth much fruit. He who loves his life, will lose it, and he who hates his life in this world, will keep it unto life everlasting. If anyone is to be my servant, he must follow me; and where I am there also shall my servant be. If anyone serves me, my Father will honor him" (John 12:24–6).

"What thou thyself sowest is not brought to life unless it dies: and what thou sowest is not the full body that is one day to be. It is only grain. . . . But God gives it a body according to his will, to each grain the body that belongs to it" (I Cor. 15:36–7).

THE WHOLE STORY of our redemption is reflected in the life of the grain of wheat, which is sown in a furrow and buried in the earth. Dying in darkness, it sends its roots into the ground to secure a solid footing. Out of the depths it rises high into the air, bearing fruit a hundredfold. At harvest time it is cut and brought to the threshing floor. There the good wheat is separated from the chaff, and stored in barns until it is brought to the mill and ground into flour. Thus the grain dies only to live again; it is destroyed only to become useful.

The symbol of the ear of wheat played an important role in the mysteries which were celebrated at Eleusis in honor of the goddess Demeter. At their climax, an ear of wheat was harvested in deep silence. It was considered as a symbol of the constant self-renewal of vegetative life. In the light of Christ, the grain of wheat represents the life-giving power of God's sacrificial love, which through Christ conquers death by death. The parable of the grain which dies to bring forth much fruit, instead of expressing the aspiration of pagan civilization for a life without death and without sacrifice, inaugurates rather the new spring of the Church which arises out of the tomb of Christ.

The single grain sown in the ground is the Word

of God sent by the Divine Sower to the earth to become Man, to die and to be buried. This Divine Seed spreads its roots deep into the earth when it descends into hell. After three days it rises, not alone, but with many brethren.

The ears of wheat are the faithful, born through the death of Christ. They remain within the protective hull of the Church until the harvest day of Judgment, when the wheat and the chaff, the good and the bad, are separated, the latter to be burned in hell, and the former to be stored in the barns of heaven. But until this last harvest and separation the faithful will share the fate of their Master; they will be cast into the furrows of the earth which will hate and destroy them. If they love life and use it for selfish ends they will lose it in eternal life; if they hate it, and prefer to lose it rather than the grace of Christ, they will keep it unto life eternal, and their blood will become the seed of the Church. The grain dying only to live, and disintegrating only to become useful, is symbolic of that divine selfless love which, in the Head and in the members of Christ's Body, dies that the dead may live.

The Bread of Life

"I am the bread of life. Your fathers ate manna in the desert, and yet they died. The bread which comes down from heaven is such that one eats of it and never dies. I am the living bread that has come down from heaven. If anyone eats of this bread, he shall live forever; and more, the bread that I will give is my flesh, given for the life of the world" (John 6:48–51).

"Is not the bread we break a participation in the body of the Lord? Because there is one bread, we, many as we are, are one body, for we all share the one bread" (I Cor. 10:16–17).

———•—◆—•———

GOD, like a loving and provident father, feeds his children with the Bread of Life. At the heavenly banquet his Son is the Bread of the angels who, in loving contemplation, feed on the Word of God. When God chose Israel to take the place of the angels on earth, he fed them with manna from heaven (Exod. 16:4), and a table was put into the Tabernacle with twelve loaves of bread, according to the number of the tribes of Israel (Lev. 24:5–7). The manna and the bread stand not only for earthly food, but are symbols of the Law, which is called, "bread for those who seek after wisdom" (cf. Heb. 6:5).

The Law of God is the Word of God. The manna from heaven and the bread in the Tabernacle upon which God would always fix his gaze were symbols of the Word of God made flesh: Jesus Christ. He is the Divine Wisdom who in the Old Testament furnishes the people with bread and wine and sends out invitations to the feast. "Wisdom hath built herself a house, she hath hewn out her seven pillars: She hath killed her calves; she hath mingled her wine; she hath also furnished her table. She hath sent forth her maidens to the tower, and on the walls of the city she crieth: 'Whosoever is a little one, let him come to me,' and to the unwise she said: 'Come, eat my bread, and drink the wine which I have mingled for you. Forsake childishness, and live, and walk by the ways of prudence' " (Prov. 9:1–6). At the Last Supper he takes bread into his hands and changes it into his very Body to give it to his Church as daily bread on her voyage to heaven. The Bread of the angels has become the Bread of men! All those who partake of the one loaf become one body in Christ, children of their Heavenly Father, brethren of one another.

Through Christ the faithful themselves become the "bread of Christ." Like the grains they are gathered together from all the parts of the earth through the preaching of the Gospel. The shell of their selfishness is broken in penance and suffering. The water of Baptism forms them into one mass of dough, which, in turn, is made into one loaf by the fire of the Holy Spirit received in Confirmation. The bread that is offered at Holy Mass is, therefore, a symbol of the faithful, who, eager to share in the sacrifice of Christ, say with St. Ignatius of Antioch: "I am the wheat of God, and I must be ground by the teeth of the lions that I may become the pure bread of Christ."

The Precious Pearl

"Do not give that which is holy to the dogs, neither throw your pearls before pigs or they will trample them under their feet and tear you to pieces" (Matt. 7:6).

"Again, the kingdom of heaven is like a merchant in search of fine pearls. He found one precious pearl, and went and sold everything he had, and bought it" (Matt. 13:45–6).

"And the twelve gates were twelve single pearls, one pearl for each gate" (Apoc. 21:21).

THE MYSTERY of the pearl has captured the imagination of man from time immemorial. How can the flesh of the oyster produce a gem as white, as solid, as round as a pearl? Although born in the darkness of the ocean, it shines brightly with the silvery luster of the sky. An old legend says that in the early hours of a day in spring the oyster comes to the surface of the sea, opens her shell, and receives the heavenly dew that descends from the sun, the moon and the stars. Thus it conceives the pearl, which then grows, and finally is detached from the flesh of the oyster without hurting it.

Another version of this legend attributes the origin of the pearl to the lightning descending into the ocean during a thunderstorm. The mixture of fire and water enters the oyster and produces the pearl. The lightning is Zeus, the highest of the gods, who in the depth of the ocean begets Venus, the goddess of love, whose image or *typus* is the pearl. A shell brings the newborn Venus to the shore.[1]

Nearly all the Fathers applied the legend to Christ.[2] It offered a striking similarity to the Incarnation of the Word of God who was conceived of the heavenly dew of the Holy Ghost in the womb of the Virgin Mary. She, in turn, was often compared to the shell. This was the reason why the Christians of old decorated the conch in the apse of a church in the form of a shell, beneath which, on the altar, the Pearl was born again through the words of consecration. As the pearl is raised from the depths of the ocean high into the crowns of kings, so Christ ascended from the depths of the grave to be set, as the most precious pearl, in the eternal crown of the Heavenly Father.[3]

The very shape [4] of the pearl is, and always will be, an image of the Word of God made man. He is solid as a pearl in the immutability of eternity, white in the holiness of life, bright with the light of Divine Truth, having the smoothness of meekness and the infinite worth of blessedness. Round through the possession of all perfection, the Divine Word reveals the glory of God and again may be compared to the pearl, that, as St. Ephrem says, "is all face." That is the reason, too, why the gates of the New Jerusalem are said to be formed of a single pearl. The Word of God is the door to salvation.

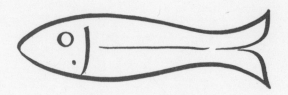

Fish of the Living

"Fishermen shall stand on the shore, and shall spread their nets on it, and fish of all kinds shall be plentiful" (Ezek. 47:10).

"When they landed they saw a fire burning, with a fish on it, and some bread. Jesus said to them: 'Bring some of the fish you have just caught.' So Simon Peter got into the boat, and hauled the net ashore, full of large fish, a hundred and fifty-three of them, and with all that number the net had not broken. Jesus said to them: 'Come and have breakfast.' None of the disciples dared to ask him who he was, for they knew it was the Master. Jesus went and took the bread and gave it to them, and the fish as well. This was now the third time that Jesus showed himself to his disciples after he was risen from the dead" (John 21:9–14).

———•◆•———

EVER SINCE GOD said: "Let the waters swarm with swarms of living creatures" (Gen. 1:20), the sea, the lakes, and the streams have teemed with shoals of fish and "fry innumerable," so that the fish has become a symbol of inexhaustible vitality. Diving into the dark recesses of the waters, "the fish swims, but is never drowned" (St. Ambrose).

It is generally believed that the symbol of the fish is a Christian invention, and that it is derived from the fact that the letters of the Greek word for fish, *Ichthys,* are an abbreviation of the name and the titles of Christ: *"Iesous CHristos THeou Yios Soter—* Jesus Christ, God's Son, Saviour." However, this derivation is of later origin, and is only one of the factors which contributed to the popularity of the symbol. The fish had been venerated long before, all over the Mediterranean area, as a symbol of luck, of life, and of fertility; especially in Syria, where it was sacred to the goddess of love. As the grain of wheat, which is sown into the ground and rises again, was held sacred in the cult of Ceres as a kind of life-giving sacrament for mortal men, so was the fish, which lives in the dark depth of the sea but often rises to the surface, considered as wielding power over the regions of death, helping the deceased to rise again to the light. Only the fish with scales and fins rise up to the light and air. Those without them, such as eels, cling to the mud of the river bed. For this reason, only the former were considered "pure," and only they could be offered as sacrifice or eaten in holy repasts in memory of the deceased (cf. Lev. 11:10). This explains the frequent use of the fish symbol on tombstones and on representations of memorial meals on both pagan and Christian monuments. It reminded the Christians of the saving power of their Lord, who, having conquered death, gave his body and his blood, the "medicine of immortality," to his followers in the sacrament of Holy Eucharist. To them the fish was a symbol, not of the dead, as it was to the pagans, but of the Risen Christ, truly the "Fish of the living," as we read on the inscription of a Christian tombstone dating from the second century.[1]

Christ is the Fish. He is typified in the "big fish" which the young Tobias catches in the river Tigris, whose flesh he roasts to sustain him on his journey, whose heart he uses to drive away the demons and whose gall cures the blind (Tob. 6:2). The true meaning of the fish in Tobias 6 is obscured by the Vulgate, which translates it *piscis immanis,* rendered by the Douay version as "monstrous fish." The Greek text has *ichthys megas,* which means "big fish." In Greco-Roman antiquity people made a distinction between "big fish," which were very expensive, and formed the pride of the tables of the rich, and "small fish," which were the cheap nourishment of the poor. "Big fish" were served only at meals of a festive character, especially on Easter Sunday and at Christmas. The custom of having fish on days of abstinence is of later origin.[2]

The Son of God made man is the "heavenly fish," the "pure one which the Virgin caught." These quotations are taken from the inscriptions of Abercius and of Pectorius, which probably go back to the third century. He hid himself in the recess of this mortal nature. He was lifted up from the basin of the Jordan at his Baptism, laid upon the coals of sufferings on the Cross. He dived into the dark region of death, but swiftly rose again into the light. After his Resurrection he gave himself as life-giving nourishment to his disciples.

Now he is present in the baptismal font, where the faithful are born as the "little fish of Christ." Swimming in the stormy waters of this world, they are caught up in the net of apostolic preaching, and hooked on the line of salvation through the sweet bait of the Son of God made man. They are reborn in the waters of Baptism. They are the "fish of every kind" that Ezechiel saw swimming in the mighty river which in the Messianic age springs forth from under the threshold of the Temple (Ezek. 47). This mighty river which rushes through the desert to the brackish waters of the Dead Sea, and, by entering, turns them into fresh water, is the Spirit poured out by the Messias. Fishermen stand all along the shore, spreading their nets and catching fish of every kind. In John 21 we see the fishermen of the Messianic age, the disciples of Christ, at work on the shores of Lake Tiberias. The number of one hundred fifty-three big fish caught by them means one of each kind, because one hundred fifty-three was the number of species of fish known at that time. The unbroken net indicates the unity in the universality of the Church. When Jesus orders the disciples to bring some of the fish which they have caught to add them to the one that is already on the fire, he points to the mystery of the Eucharist, wherein the sacrifice of the faithful is united to that of Christ. He also alludes to the day when, drawn in the unbreakable net of the Church to the shores of eternity, the little fish of the faithful will be united forever with Christ, the Fish of the Living.

Alpha and Omega

———•—•—•———

"Thus says the Lord, the King of Israel and his Redeemer, the Lord of hosts: 'I am the First, and I
am the Last, and beside me there is no God'" (Isa.
44:6).

"I am the first and the last and the Living One. I
was dead, and behold, I am living evermore" (Apoc.
1:18).

"Behold, I come quickly! And my reward is with me,
to render to each one according to his works. I am the

Alpha and the Omega, the first and the last, the beginning and the end" (Apoc. 22:12-13).

SYMBOLS, as a rule, should not be "made"; they are, rather, "found" in the things God has presented in the great picture book of his visible creation. But a symbol representing the One who reaches from one end of creation to the other, filling all things, cannot be found among earthly forms. God himself gave us such a sign when he said: "I am the Alpha and the Omega, the beginning and the end, who is and who was and who is coming" (Apoc. 1:8). The first and last letters of the Greek alphabet are chosen to denote the Lord God, who is the First, because there is no God before him, and the Last, because there is no God after him. He is, therefore, the only One who embraces all of creation and all of human history, with whom alone it began, and with whom alone it will end.

The symbolism of the first and the last letter of the alphabet is, in all probability, of Jewish origin. The Jew is the man of the letter, because the letters are the "elements" which make up what is to him the one and only universal manifestation of God's wisdom, the Law. The ideal of the Jew is, therefore, to fulfill the Law "from Aleph to Tau." [1]

In the New Testament, the Alpha and Omega became a symbol of Christ in whom the course of human history is summed up. As Tertullian says (*On Monogamy,* chap. 5): "The two letters of the Greek alphabet, the first and the last, the Lord assumes to himself, so that, just as Alpha rolls on till it reaches Omega, and again, Omega rolls back till it reaches Alpha, in the same way he might show that in himself is both the downward course of the beginning to the end, and the backward course of the end up to the beginning; so that every economy, ending in him through whom it began—through the Word of God, that is, who was made flesh—may have an end corresponding to its beginning." [2]

The Alpha and the Omega declare that he who was made man at the end of time is the same through whom all things were made in the beginning. The Son of God made man is the First who became the Last. He descended into the lower parts of this earth, and then ascended to the heights above the heavens so that he might fill all things, becoming the "Head," the beginning and the end of a New Creation, the "Yes" and the "Amen" to all the promises of God. The Alpha and the Omega is, therefore, the symbol of the Lamb slain from the foundation of the world, the Eternal Love which foreordains us into adoption as sons, which reaches not only from the beginning to the end, but extends as well from the heights of divine perfection to the abyss of human frailty. It is a universal invitation to contemplate the end in the light of the beginning, and to rest assured that "mercy first and last shall brightest shine."

Notes

THE SEAL OF THE LIVING GOD

1. On the mark on Cain's forehead, cf. Bernhard Stade, "Das Kainszeichen," *Zeitschrift für Alttestamentliche Wissenschaft*, XIV (1894), 250 *et seq.*
2. Rufinus, *Historia Ecclesiastica*, II, 26; cf. Photina Rech, O.S.B., "Die Lebensbotschaft einer aegyptischen Hieroglyphe," Herbstbrief der Abtei Herstelle (1949), 31.
3. cf. A. Jeremias, *Handbuch der Altorientalischen Geisteskultur* (Leipzig, 1929), pp. 192 ff.
4. J. S. Brown (ed.), *The Sacred Pipe* (Norman, Oklahoma: University of Oklahoma Press, 1953), p. 59.
5. cf. Hugo Rahner, "Das Schiff aus Kreuzholz," *Zeitschrift für Katholische Theologie* 67 (1943), 1–21.
6. On the identity of ladder and cross cf. Eleanor Simmons Greenhill, "The Child in the Tree," *Traditio* X (New York: Fordham University Press, 1954), 343–49.
7. The most complete collection of all scriptural material on the cross is given in J. Gretser, *De Sancta Cruce* (Regensburg, 1734). More recent is the classical study of Hugo Rahner, "Das Mysterium des Kreuzes," in *Griechische Mythen in christlicher Deutung* (Zurich, Rhein Verlag, 1945), 73–100; and the above-mentioned article by Eleanor Simmons Greenhill. The spiritual meaning of the cross in the life of the Christian and throughout the holy year of the Church is beautifully expounded by Odo Casel in *Mysterium des Kreuzes* (Paderborn, 1954).

THE TREE OF LIFE

1. cf. J. G. Frazer, *The Golden Bough* (abridged ed., New York, 1942), pp. 120 ff.
2. cf. Tiele, *Yule and Christmas* (London, 1899).
3. cf. Mircea Eliade, "Psychology and Comparative Religion: A Study of the Symbolism of the Centre," in *Selection II* (New York: Sheed & Ward, 1954), p. 29.

Notes

4. J. E. Brown, *op. cit.*, pp. 73–81.
5. cf. Strack-Billerbeck, *Kommentar zum Neuen Testament aus Talmud und Midrasch,* IV, p. 51.
6. cf. Eleanor Simmons Greenhill, *op. cit.*, pp. 338 *et seq.;* Hugo Rahner, *op. cit.*, p. 93; René Guénon, "L'Arbre du Milieu," *Le Symbolisme de la Croix* (Paris, 1931), chap. 9; Odo Casel, "Der neue Baum des Lebens," *op. cit.*, p. 52, quoting Anastasius Sinaita, "The Cross of Christ Is the Tree of Life."
7. cf. Genesis 28:12; cf. E. S. Greenhill, *loc. cit.*, pp. 343–49.
8. cf. St. Benedict, *The Holy Rule,* chap. 7.
9. cf. "Homélies Pascales, Une Homélie inspirée du Trâité sur la Pâque," in *Sources Chrétiennes,* XXVII (1950), 176–78; English translation in Henri de Lubac, *Catholicism* (New York: Longmans, Green & Co., 1950), p. 282.

THE HOLY MOUNTAIN

1. cf. A. Jeremias, *The Old Testament in the Light of the Ancient East* (1911), I, p. 54; G. Van der Leeuw, *Phaenomenologie der Religion* (Tübingen, 1933), pp. 34 *et sqq.;* article "oros" in *Theologisches Wörterbuch zum Neuen Testament,* V, 475 *et sqq.;* Mircea Eliade, *loc. cit.*, Selection II, 30–1.
2. Ben Gurion, *Die Sagen der Juden* (1927), p. 182.

THE BURNING BUSH

1. The Hebrew "Sené" is a thornbush, probably a kind of hawthorn. The Vulgate translates "rubus"—bramble bush.

THE STAR OF JACOB

1. *Sources Chrétiennes, loc. cit.,* 116–18.

THE ROD OF JESSE

1. cf. E. Zolli, *The Nazarene* (St. Louis, Missouri, 1950), pp. 7–60, for further explanation of this term.

THE KEY OF DAVID

1. cf. Joachim Jeremias, "kleis," in *Theologisches Wörterbuch,* III, 743–53; O. Cullman, *Saint Pierre* (Neuchâtel, 1952). Both authors show the great change which recently has

taken place in Protestant exegesis toward a more "Catholic" interpretation of the crucial passage Matt. 16:16–19.

THE CORNERSTONE

1. Joachim Jeremias, "Der Eckstein," in *Angelos* I (1925), 65 ff.
2. *Theologisches Wörterbuch*, I, 792–93; A. K. Coomeraswamy, "Eckstein," in *Speculum*, XIV, 1939, 66–72.
3. Pastor Hermae, *Similitude IX*, chap. 2, p. 1.

THE SUN OF JUSTICE

1. On Christ as "the Sun of Justice" an abundance of material is to be found in Fr. J. Doelger, *Sol Salutis*, Muenster i.W., 1925.

THE LAMB OF GOD

1. cf. Origen, *Homily in Jesus Nave*, VII, 6; St. Ambrose, *Expositio in Lucam*, VII, 209.
2. cf. J. Quasten, "The Waters of Refreshment," *The Catholic Biblical Quarterly*, I (1939), 325–32; L. S. Thornton, *The Common Life in the Body of Christ* (1944), pp. 416 ff.

THE FOUNTAIN OF LIFE

1. The oft-quoted words of John 7:38, "streams of living water shall flow from his heart," may refer either to Christ or to the believer. The alternative arises partly from an uncertainty about the punctuation. If the period is placed after "drink," the quotation refers to the faithful. If it is placed after "in me," it refers to Christ. The ambiguity is characteristic of the gospel of St. John, which throughout emphasizes the identity between Christ and the Christian. The idea that the faithful one himself turns into a spring "whose waters fail not" is clearly indicated in Isaias 58:11 (cf. Prov. 5:16; 14:27; Eccles. 24:30).

THE TRUE VINE

1. A. Jeremias, *The Old Testament in the Light of the Ancient East* (1911), I, p. 209.

Notes

2. The analogy between the vine and the *person* of Christ has been explained most beautifully by Cyrillonas, a Syrian poet of the fifth century, in his IInd Homily on the Pascha of Christ (*Syrische Dichter* [Bibliothek d. Kirchenväter], pp. 44–6). A more subjective interpretation of Christ as the Mystical Vine is offered in the famous treatise *De Vita Mystica,* falsely attributed to St. Bernard, by others to St. Bonaventure.

3. Council of Trent, session VI, chap. 16.

THE PRECIOUS PEARL

1. cf. H. Usener, "Die Perle," *Theologische Abhandlungen Weizsaeker gew* (1898), pp. 203 ff.

2. cf. Origen, *Commentary on St. Matthew,* 13:45; St. Ephrem, "On the Pearl," *Collectio Patrum,* ed. Caillau (Paris, 1835), Vol. 36, pp. 382 sqq.

3. cf. Clement of Alexandria, *Instructor,* Book II, chap. 12.

4. Among Semitic nations the pearl is often used as a symbol of a poem or a well-formed sentence. The custom of wearing pearls as earrings springs from this idea (cf. the Vulgate translation of Prov. 25:12: "As an earring of gold and a bright pearl is a wise reprover on an obedient ear").

FISH OF THE LIVING

1. cf. Fr. J. Doelger, *Ichthys,* Vol. II (Muenster l.w. 1922).

2. cf. Tertullian, *On Baptism,* I; Inscription of Aberkius "a fish from the fountain, a big fish, and pure."

3. cf. Rev. H. P. V. Nunn, M.A., *Christian Inscriptions* (New York, 1952), pp. 28–32.

ALPHA AND OMEGA

1. cf. F. Dornseiff, *Das Alphabet in Mystik und Magie* (1925); A. Schlatter, *Das Alte Testament in der johanneischen Apokalypse* (1912); Kittel, *Theologisches Wörterbuch,* I, s.v.AO.

2. Other Fathers explaining the AO: Clement of Alexandria, *Stromata,* IV, 141; Primasius Hadrum., *Commentary to the Apocalypse* V, chap. 22; Migne, *Patrologia Latina,* 68, col. 932; Prudentius, Hymn. 9 Cathem.